Fair Hair, Dark Hair

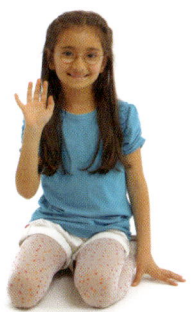

Written by
Stephen Rickard

This is Yasmin.

Yasmin has dark hair.
Can you see her dark hair?

Her dark hair is not short.

This is Yasmin's mum.

Yasmin's mum has dark hair too.
Can you see her dark hair?

Her hair is not fair.

This is Yasmin's dad.

Yasmin's dad has dark hair.
Can you see his dark hair?

Can you see his ears?

No! I cannot see his ears.
His hair is not short.

Yasmin's dad has a beard as well.

Can you see his beard?

He has dark hair and a dark beard.

This is Zak.

Zak has fair hair.
Can you see his fair hair?

Has Zak got a beard?

This is Zak's mum.

Zak's mum has fair hair too.
Can you see her fair hair?

Has Zak's mum got short hair?

Has Zak's mum got a beard?

Look in this mirror.

Can you see much?

Can you see you?

Can you see dark hair or fair hair?

Yes! This has to be you!

I cannot see dark hair
and I cannot see fair hair.

But I can see red fur!